Rialto
Mortmain
Dead End

Three Plays

by

Richard Parsons

Samuel French — London
New York - Toronto - Hollywood

Copyright © 1993 by Richard Parsons
All Rights Reserved

RIALTO, MORTMAIN, DEAD END is fully protected under the copyright laws of the British Commonwealth, including Canada, the United States of America, and all other countries of the Copyright Union. All rights, including professional and amateur stage productions, recitation, lecturing, public reading, motion picture, radio broadcasting, television and the rights of translation into foreign languages are strictly reserved.

ISBN 978-0-573-10001-7

www.samuelfrench.co.uk
www.samuelfrench.com

> **FOR AMATEUR PRODUCTION ENQUIRIES**
>
> **UNITED KINGDOM AND WORLD EXCLUDING NORTH AMERICA**
> plays@samuelfrench.co.uk
> 020 7255 4302/01
>
> Each title is subject to availability from Samuel French, depending upon country of performance.

CAUTION: Professional and amateur producers are hereby warned that RIALTO, MORTMAIN, DEAD END is subject to a licensing fee. Publication of this play does not imply availability for performance. Both amateurs and professionals considering a production are strongly advised to apply to the appropriate agent before starting rehearsals, advertising, or booking a theatre. A licensing fee must be paid whether the title is presented for charity or gain and whether or not admission is charged.

The Professional Rights in this play are controlled by Peters Fraser and Dunlop Limited, 503/4 The Chambers, Chelsea Harbour, Lots Road, London SW10 OXF.

No one shall make any changes in this title for the purpose of production. No part of this book may be reproduced, stored in a retrieval system, or transmitted in any form, by any means, now known or yet to be invented, including mechanical, electronic, photocopying, recording, videotaping, or otherwise, without the prior written permission of the publisher. No one shall upload this title, or part of this title, to any social media websites.

The right of Richard Parsons to be identified as author of this work has been asserted in accordance with Section 77 of the Copyright, Designs and Patents Act 1988.

RIALTO, MORTMAIN and DEAD END

	Page
RIALTO	1
MORTMAIN	21
DEAD END	37
Furniture and property lists, lighting and effects plots	47

RIALTO

CHARACTERS

Bruce A man of about forty-five or fifty. Reasonably educated voice. He sounds bold and confident but can begin to crumble under pressure. There is a certain seediness about him which slowly becomes apparent.

Clemmie A widow lady, rather older than Bruce but still not without mature attraction. Prosperous middle-class from the commuter belt. At first she seems out of her depth but gradually an element of inner steeliness emerges.

A licence issued by Samuel French Ltd to perform this play does not include permission to use the incidental music specified in this copy. Where the place of performance is already licensed by the PERFORMING RIGHT SOCIETY a return of the music used must be made to them. If the place of performance is not so licensed then application should be made to the PERFORMING RIGHT SOCIETY, 29 Berners Street, London W1

A separate and additional licence from PHONOGRAPHIC PERFORMANCES LTD, Ganton House, Ganton Street, London W1 is needed whenever commercial recordings are used.

RIALTO

First presented at the King's Head Theatre, Islington on 16 January, 1992 by Sydney Golder for Elephant Theatre with the following cast:

Bruce   Anthony Gardner
Clemmie   Anne Robson

Directed by Sylvia Denning

RIALTO

It is early summer in Venice. We hear the bustle of the town. Bruce and Clemmie are sitting at a table out of doors, at a lively café near the Rialto Bridge

Bruce I hope you're enjoying it.
Clemmie Every minute. I'm determined to.
Bruce Good. That was the idea.
Clemmie I love the sitting out. You can't do that in Amersham.
Bruce You can't always do it here. Venice can be horribly dank in winter. All that water.
Clemmie I shouldn't like it here in high summer either. I don't brown very well.
Bruce That's why we chose May. Before the tourist flood. Those awful gangs of Japanese at the Accademia.
Clemmie Wasn't that where we saw all the pictures? The Titian and the Tintoretto. Where I had to take my shoes off in the Ladies.
Bruce I was sorry about your feet.
Clemmie I'm fond of pictures. Though not too many at a time.
Bruce I'll remember that, Mrs Wyndham-White.
Clemmie I do wish you'd call me Clemmie. We've been here for three days.
Bruce Clemmie?
Clemmie I don't care for Clementina. Such a mouthful.
Bruce All right. But then you must call me Bruce.

Clemmie I like Bruce. Such a manly, outdoors name.
Bruce That's what my parents wanted me to be.
Clemmie I expect they were proud of you. Didn't you say you acted in the West End?
Bruce That was ages ago. I was quite in demand for juvenile parts. I had a strong profile, especially from the left.
Clemmie Then you wrote novels. That's what you told me.
Bruce There's not much money in that. I was never in paperback.
Clemmie You must have had an interesting life.
Bruce (*dryly*) It's not quite over yet.
Clemmie I'm sorry. I do say clumsy things, don't I? Since my husband died, I've been alone rather a lot, doing the garden. That can make you seem insensitive.
Bruce I don't think you're insensitive. You're rather nice.
Clemmie You're a gallant man, Bruce. Like the Italians. I had my first pinch this morning.
Bruce Where?
Clemmie Where would you expect? Oh, I see. In Saint Mark's of all places. You warned me that Italians would pinch. You used that as an argument for me not having this holiday alone.
Bruce Many Italian men like to show their appreciation of the female form. Sometimes they go too far.
Clemmie That's the trouble in Amersham. We never do.
Bruce The change will do you good. Would you like some more coffee — er — Clemmie?
Clemmie No, thank you. I'm glad to take the weight off my feet. You seem to choose resting places with such splendid views.
Bruce That's not difficult in this city. Over there is the famous Rialto Bridge. I often think of that as the real heart of Venice.
Clemmie Not Saint Mark's Square with all the pigeons? Or the Doge's Palace?
Bruce That's the ceremonial centre, of course. But the Venetians were traders. All through the centuries. That's how they could afford to subsidize Monteverdi and Vivaldi. They sat on the trade route to the East and they made their pile. The deals were done right here on the Rialto. Just think of all that buying cheap and selling dear. Both sides wanting the best possible bargain. Each hoping to produce a joker from up his sleeve. That's what the Rialto means to me.
Clemmie But that's not how they describe Venice in the tourist leaflets.

Bruce Oh no, it's supposed to be a city of culture. Maybe it is, these days. But that's half way to stagnation. I prefer to think of the old mercantile Venice, a trading empire based on the sea, just as we used to be in England.

Clemmie I expect my husband would have agreed with you. He was an accountant, you know. He specialized in corporate bankruptcies. It's a growth area. In the City they called him The Vulture. But that was only a joke. We used to take holidays at hot spots with small beaches. Corfu, Ibiza, Lanzarote. The others loved it.

Bruce But you pined for a little culture?

Clemmie Not really. I just had this problem with going brown. I looked like a lobster for much of the time. But Vincent needed the break. That was my husband. He had to uncoil. Otherwise he might have snapped.

Bruce You must miss him very much.

Clemmie I did at first. I thought I would never get over it. But then, you know, I began to recover. To my surprise. I was so busy with the Red Cross. And the campaign to keep the Chilterns green. Sometimes now I go through whole days without thinking of Vincent at all. That makes me feel quite guilty.

Bruce I shouldn't worry. I expect your husband would be glad.

Clemmie You didn't know Vincent. He liked to be the centre of attention.

Bruce I'm sure you were a good wife.

Clemmie I'd like to think I was. But now I'm concentrating on being a good widow.

Bruce It's so unfair, isn't it? Widows are expected to be mournful. Why shouldn't they be merry?

Clemmie (*coolly*) I'm no merry widow, Bruce. You seem to forget that I'm expecting to die soon.

Bruce I'm sorry. You appear to be much alive.

Clemmie I try to be while I am.

Bruce My wife was very vivacious. I expect she still is.

Clemmie In New Zealand, you told me.

Bruce She went home to Mother.

Clemmie I'm sorry for you that it didn't work out.

Bruce It was a tremendous relief to get rid of her. She smoked in bed.

Clemmie Vincent flaked out at the end of each day. They drained him at the office. He had a wonderful head for figures.

Bruce Miranda was just the opposite. The money slipped through her fingers.

Clemmie Italians are awfully talkative, aren't they? Look at that fat lady, the way she's moving her whole body to express a point.
Bruce They're different from us. That's the charm of Italy.
Clemmie I couldn't have managed it alone. Vincent used to cope with the money and the passports. I just sat on the luggage and waited for the next thing to happen.
Bruce Your children must have been a great help to you. After you lost him.
Clemmie They did their best. But my daughter Shirley is married, you know, and my son is rather up in the clouds.
Bruce It's not easy being a parent, is it? (*He sighs*) One has problems.
Clemmie Tell me about them.
Bruce Some other time perhaps. I don't want to be a bore. It's my job to entertain *you*.
Clemmie Oh, and you do. I like your enthusiasm. Not only for the guide book things. But for the idea of Venice. You don't seem to notice the smells.
Bruce They came here first to be safe, you know. From the barbarians on the mainland.
Clemmie It doesn't seem specially safe here now. There's no proper drainage.
Bruce Death in Venice and all that.
Clemmie I'm not including that in my plans.
Bruce Next year we could go somewhere else. Amalfi is still charming.
Clemmie Next year I may be dead.
Bruce I'll tell you what, Clemmie. You need a stiff drink before dinner. It should be just about warm enough to sit out on the balcony of the hotel. Watch the steamers coming in from the Lido.
Clemmie And that lovely church on the other side of the Grand Canal. What's it called again?
Bruce Santa Maria della Salute. It looks best from a distance.
Clemmie Don't we all?
Bruce You look very nice from close up.
Clemmie You don't have to say things like that, Bruce. It's not in the contract.
Bruce I may be running a business but I'm still an artist.
Clemmie Let's take a gondola back to the hotel.
Bruce They're awfully expensive.
Clemmie Expense is no object. I can't take it with me. I explained that to

you when I first answered your advertisement.
Bruce I was nervous about advertising. Didn't want to give the wrong impression. About the service I offer.
Clemmie What you offer is perfectly clear. I'm surprised that nobody had thought of it before. (*She shouts*) Hallo. It worked, Bruce. He's coming into the landing stage to pick up. Don't you adore his dark, curly hair?
Bruce I expect he has it permed. Gondoliers are a branch of show business nowadays.

A hoot as the vaporetto passes them on its way down the Grand Canal. Watery gurgles as they climb into the gondola. In this, as in the other intermissions, we hear music particularly associated with Venice such as the Barcarolle from the "Tales of Hoffmann"

Cut to another outdoor scene. Seagulls on the Venetian lagoon

Clemmie It was a good idea. Coming out here to Torcello for the day.
Bruce The ultimate refuge. The furthest corner of the Lagoon.
Clemmie I didn't know there would be such a good restaurant here for lunch.
Bruce I don't like to miss my meals.
Clemmie Nor do I. There won't be so many more of them.
Bruce You upset me when you talk like that.
Clemmie Why should that upset you? You knew it from the start.
Bruce I suppose I'm getting to like you, Clemmie.
Clemmie Do you say that to all your clients?
Bruce As a matter of fact, you are only my third.
Clemmie What happened to the others?
Bruce One is living very quietly in a home in Somerset.
Clemmie And the other?
Bruce She — er — passed on. Shortly after our lovely holiday together in Marrakesh. I'm glad she saw the snake charmers.
Clemmie Elderly women, I suppose?
Bruce Well, why not? They are the ones who find themselves stranded.
Clemmie One doesn't get invited out much. As a woman alone. Thank heavens Vincent made money.
Bruce Would you like to go into the cathedral now? Such a grand name for a lonely little Byzantine church.
Clemmie I'd rather talk to you. It interests me. This business of yours.

Bruce It seems to answer a need.
Clemmie What made you start it?
Bruce I was rather at a loose end. And I wanted the money.
Clemmie There must have been more to it than that.
Bruce All right. I suppose I've always been rather interested in the winter of life. The hospice movement is based on the assumption that the last few months don't have to be a misery. I thought that concept could be extended further. There must be a fair number of people, I guessed, who knew they were going to die soon and were determined to do it in style. I set out to help them.
Clemmie Isn't that rather a macabre idea?
Bruce Not to me. The clients are so charming.
Clemmie You mean they tend to be on their best behaviour because they know they haven't got long?
Bruce I expect you were nice. Even before.
Clemmie I'm not all that nice. I don't love my children as much as I should.
Bruce There's no need for guilt. These terminal weeks could be wonderfully serene. No need to bother about sending in an income tax return. No more worries over the stock market. Let the garage roof go to pot.
Clemmie And eating chocolate. I don't fuss any more about my figure.
Bruce It's a very nice figure. Considering.
Clemmie Considering what? My advanced age?
Bruce I mean, with your illness. This last week, I've been wondering how you could look so healthy and eat so well.
Clemmie I told you. I'm hanging on to life. Like a rock climber marooned on a ledge.
Bruce Your children would want you to make the best of it.
Clemmie They don't care all that much.
Bruce I don't believe that.
Clemmie I'm not encouraging them to get dramatic. Shirley is so busy with their new home in Guildford. And now she's got the baby. Truth to tell, I never have been all that close to Michael. That's my son-in-law. He keeps looking at me as if I had said something stupid. Even when I haven't.
Bruce But you have a son too.
Clemmie Rupert. A very loving boy. But he never manages to get his act together. He keeps forgetting birthdays and then they cut off his phone

when he hasn't paid the bill. You can't rely on a person like that. I wanted children who would be sure to be with me at the end. I'm frightened of having to go off all alone.

Bruce It's a thing you have to do on your own. But there's no point in thinking about it now. Would you like an ice-cream? In Italy they make the best in the world.

Clemmie I don't feel like an ice-cream. I just want to go on sitting here. Watching the birds and sky. While I can.

Bruce That's the whole idea. I put it in my brochure. Make it the holiday of a lifetime.

Clemmie I shall clock in everything possible. While the poor old body lasts. When we get home to England, I'll take a short rest. And then I think I'll fly to New York on Concorde. And from there to California. De luxe, of course.

Bruce That costs real money.

Clemmie It doesn't matter. Vincent worked hard all his life to provide for me. I have every right to spend it.

Bruce Your children must be upset.

Clemmie About me getting rid of the money?

Bruce I meant, about what the specialist told you.

Clemmie Shirley and Michael took me to Harley Street. They sat in the waiting room while I went in to receive the sentence. When I came out, I didn't want to talk about it. But, when we got stuck in a traffic jam at Marble Arch, I told them quite simply that it was malignant and I hadn't got long.

Bruce How awful.

Clemmie They were surprisingly brave. Almost too brave. Michael wrote me a tactful letter advising me to put my affairs in order. I knew what he meant. He doesn't miss much, does Master Michael. That encouraged me to think about myself. Just for once. And then I saw your advertisement, offering to help people approach the end of their lives with a bang rather than a whimper. I took to the idea at once. But it can't be much fun for you.

Bruce On the contrary. Women without earthly cares can be extremely entertaining. We've had some good giggles.

Clemmie When you smile like that, you look rather a saucy old thing.

Bruce I try to be professional. Even with the most attractive clients.

Clemmie You're a dark horse, Bruce. That's one of the things I like about you. When we talk about children, you seem to sigh as if you had a hidden sorrow. But you never come out with it.

Bruce I didn't feel able to before. But now we've become friends, haven't we?

Clemmie We certainly have.

Bruce Well, I'll tell you. There *is* something rather sad about both my children.

Clemmie Are they in New Zealand, poor things?

Bruce No. They stayed with me in England. But now they are horribly hampered.

Clemmie In what way?

Bruce Simon is talented. He's always been mad about music and he plays the violin like an angel. He's only thirteen and he ought to go now to a special school for gifted children.

Clemmie Well, why not?

Bruce I haven't got the money.

Clemmie Can't he get a scholarship?

Bruce They're cutting down on all that these days. It's dreadful to me to think that his career is going to be blighted, just for lack of a little cash.

Clemmie And what about the other one?

Bruce Melissa, my daughter. Only ten and so sweet. But she had an accident in early childhood. Now she can hardly walk. If only she could have a hip operation, they would be able to cure her. Then she could run about like the other children.

Clemmie How very sad. She ought to have that operation as soon as possible.

Bruce That's what the surgeon says. But again I haven't the money.

Clemmie Couldn't she have it for free?

Bruce There is a long waiting list. It's hell, you know, being poor.

Clemmie I know. I was poor once too. Long ago. Before Vincent took up bankruptcies. That was the making of us. He had a talent for the paper work.

Bruce I'm sorry. The misfortunes of my family are not very inspiring.

Clemmie Not at all, Bruce. I sympathize with all three of you. It must be tough, watching your children suffer.

Bruce It's something I have to live with.

Clemmie You ought to get hold of some money. From those rich women you escort around in their last weeks.

Bruce (*stung*) Mrs Wyndham-White, I'm surprised at you. What a thing to say.

Clemmie It just slipped out.
Bruce You made me tell you. I didn't want to, as you will remember. That's the horrible thing about being poor. One's motives are always suspect.
Clemmie I'm sorry. It was my silly idea of a joke.
Bruce I still feel rather hurt.
Clemmie You must forgive me. I haven't got long.
Bruce All right. But don't let's talk about my children ever again.
Clemmie Now that you have told me, I insist on doing something for both of them. They sound charming and promising. And the mother so far away.
Bruce Now you're embarrassing me, Clemmie.
Clemmie I like to do things for other people.
Bruce I didn't mean to ask.
Clemmie Of course you didn't. That's why I want to make a gesture.
Bruce A gesture?
Clemmie Yes. You told me that the boat stops at Murano on the way back. I shall buy some ornaments there for your lovely children. You know that wonderful coloured glass they make there. Melissa shall have a bowl to keep her bits and bobs. And Simon might like another for the fiddly thing from his violin.
Bruce (*with difficulty*) You're awfully kind, Clemmie.
Clemmie Not at all. Money is for using. While one still can. I think now that I *would* like an ice-cream. A tutti-frutti perhaps. One might as well go the whole hog.

Cut to another outdoor scene. The Beach at the Lido

Sounds of the sea, children playing on the sand, a band in the distance

Bruce You're a naughty girl, Clemmie. Spending all that money.
Clemmie I thought it would be fun, coming out here to the Lido in our own motor boat.
Bruce We could have travelled in the steamer.
Clemmie With all those other people? No, thank you, I shan't be around long.
Bruce I find that increasingly difficult to believe. You look as fit as a fiddle.
Clemmie It's not how I feel. It's what's going to happen to me. Quite

soon, if the specialists are right.
Bruce They may have got it wrong.
Clemmie I hardly think so. Sir Roderick has been in Harley Street for years. He addresses conferences in Boston. Don't look so low.
Bruce I've become fond of you, Clemmie.
Clemmie I like you too, Bruce. I'm sorry to think that tomorrow will be our last day.
Bruce We'll keep in contact.
Clemmie You say that. But I know men.
Bruce I'm the loyal type. I was very touched by those large glass bowls you gave me for the children. A charming souvenir of Venetian craft work.
Clemmie I hope they won't be a nuisance in the plane. How will you carry them?
Bruce I've been thinking about that. In an airbag perhaps. They could rest on my lap.
Clemmie You might have trouble with the British customs. You know what jackals they are.
Bruce I don't expect I'll have any difficulty.
Clemmie You mean they're not worth much?
Bruce No, I didn't mean that. Not at all. Will you be buying presents for your family?
Clemmie I sent them postcards. Shirley is very fond of postcards. (*She pauses*) Oh, I know what you're thinking. I'm not much of a mother. But I haven't really forgiven Shirley and Michael.
Bruce What on earth for?
Clemmie It was rather complicated. You know how you can hate and love another person at the same time. When I told them the bad news about my health, of course they were upset. They are not monsters. They didn't want me to suffer. But I'm sure of one thing. The thought did just occur to Michael in passing that I wouldn't last long. Then they would get their share of Vincent's money.
Bruce I don't imagine that your daughter thought like that.
Clemmie Oh, but she did. He put the idea into her mind. I saw it cross her face. She's very suggestible.
Bruce You're imagining this.
Clemmie I don't really blame them. I suppose I *am* a bit of a nuisance. I like to have them over to Amersham on Sundays. It must mean a lot of extra driving for Michael on his one day off. And then they could really

do with the cash. Shirley wants a car of her own. And they like those holidays in France with lots of food and wine. They'll be sorry when I'm gone. But not all that sorry.

Bruce What about Rupert? He sounds a charmer.

Clemmie He is. It's his profession. No point in giving *him* anything. He shares a grotty flat with a group of young people who can't summon up the energy to get up in the mornings. I've been careful all my life. Vincent was that kind of man. But at last I'm enjoying spending all this money. It will only be docked off what the children inherit. And that's no skin off my nose. In fact, the thought rather amuses me. Wouldn't it be fun to go back all the way from the Lido in a gondola? You can, you know, if you're prepared to pay.

Bruce You're getting carried away, Clemmie.

Clemmie Yes, aren't I? It's like going down a slide. Tonight we'll have the best wine in the hotel. If the children could see me now, I think they'd be very distressed.

Bruce At your spending all this?

Clemmie And being in the hands of such a seductive man.

Bruce You're quite safe with me, Clemmie.

Clemmie Am I? How disappointing. You know I set you a little test.

Bruce What on earth was that?

Clemmie When I bought the Murano glass for your children. When you first told me about their problems, I thought you might be trying to get money out of me. So I inflicted on you this piffling and troublesome present to see how you would react. I was looking out for any signs of disappointment. But you took it on the chin.

Bruce (*reproachfully*) I'm not interested in money, Clemmie. You should know that by now. I'm an artist.

Clemmie I'm sorry if I misjudged you. But one can't be too sure. Lonely women like me are easy targets for the unscrupulous. Not every man is a perfect gentleman like you.

Bruce Thank you.

Clemmie I phoned my solicitor in England this morning. I've arranged to have a codicil added to my will. I'm leaving you money, Bruce. It will be more than enough to pay for your daughter's operation. And to see your boy through college.

Bruce I don't know what to say.

Clemmie Don't say anything. It makes me happy to do it.

Bruce This is wonderful, Clemmie. Such marvellous generosity. I can't begin to tell you how terribly grateful I am.

Clemmie Don't try.

Bruce You could have left it directly to my children.

Clemmie I prefer to trust *you*.

Bruce But what about your own family?

Clemmie Serve them right. You've given me a lovely holiday. I wanted to end it on a high note.

Bruce You certainly have. Darling Clemmie.

Clemmie Where shall we go tomorrow? I think we ought to repeat one of our marvellous adventures. We could go back to those villas on the Brenta.

Bruce Portia's villa. "In Belmont is a lady richly left."

Clemmie Yes, I remember you quoting that. I liked La Malcontenta best. What a sad noble woman to have a house called after her like that. I was a bit of a Malcontenta once, you know. Until I met you.

Bruce So was I. But I'm not now. (*Softly*) I'll show you tonight.

Clemmie Perhaps there will be moonlight. We could take a gondola ride after dinner. Well wrapped-up, of course. We might ask the gondolier to sing old Venetian songs.

Bruce They prefer Andrew Lloyd Webber.

Clemmie It will be an evening to remember.

Bruce I'm looking forward to the wine.

Romantic music swells. Cut to another outdoor scene. The sounds of the steamers on the Grand Canal

Clemmie I'm glad we didn't go to La Malcontenta. That house is not me anymore. Not after last night.

Bruce Last night was good.

Clemmie It wasn't good. It was wonderful.

Bruce Thank you, darling.

Clemmie I'd nearly forgotten what it could be like. Poor dear Vincent wasn't a great performer. He needed his sleep. You know, this morning, at breakfast, sitting out on the terrace, eating my croissant, I almost had difficulty looking at you straight in the face.

Bruce That's understandable.

Clemmie We've still got one more night and I don't feel embarrassed anymore. I even want to talk about it.

Bruce Those people at the next table may be listening.

Clemmie I don't care if they are. I'm not going to spend any more time now worrying about other people's reactions. Do you know, this is the same table where we sat early in our first week? Just by the Rialto Bridge. The heart of Venice, you called it. Where they pitted their wits against each other, in the buying and the selling. Life's still much the same, isn't it? We all want what we can get out of other people.
Bruce I don't know about that. Some of us are capable of acting with great generosity. You, for instance. Look what you are doing for my poor children.
Clemmie Oh, I meant to tell you. My lawyer rang again this morning. He's sent the codicil over by fax machine.
Bruce I'm most terribly grateful.
Clemmie Of course they won't get a penny until I'm dead.
Bruce I hope that won't be for a long time.
Clemmie Oh no, you don't. It's not in human nature. You want your little girl to have her operation and your boy to start at that special school for the unusually gifted.
Bruce Of course I do. But not at your expense, darling.
Clemmie There is perhaps something that I ought to explain.
Bruce You're feeling worse?
Clemmie Not at all. It's just that I find it hard to tell you. It goes back to when I had to see the man in Harley Street. That terrible day. I was in an agony of apprehension.
Bruce I can understand that, poor thing. And then hearing the awful news.
Clemmie Well, that was the point. I didn't.
Bruce You didn't?
Clemmie No. It was a ridiculous anticlimax. You see, the doctor said that my tumour was benign. I wasn't going to die. At least, not yet.
Bruce (*with an effort*) How wonderful. But why on earth did you give your family the opposite impression?
Clemmie It was naughty of me, wasn't it? But, you see, I had this idea. Between Harley Street and Marble Arch. Being fatally ill would give me a wonderful alibi. Nobody would bother me again. They wouldn't have the heart to. I could go on neglecting those nasty, brown envelopes. Rupert would stop pestering me for cash. And I could spend Vincent's money without seeming extravagant. Even Shirley and Michael could hardly object when they knew I had so little time to live.
Bruce Surely it was your money to spend as you wished.
Clemmie Not exactly. Vincent's first thought had been to leave every-

thing to the children, with me having only the life interest. He thought it would be best, tax-wise. And because I am quite keen on shopping and using credit cards. Michael liked the plan too and did his best to encourage him. That boy is a skunk.

Bruce But you outployed him.

Clemmie I'm not as stupid as I look, darling. Never have been. I got Vincent to change the will in my favour. It was after his favourite lunch, boiled beef and dumplings. I wrote out the new bit and he signed it, with the water board men as witnesses. The younger one had the sweetest little moustache. It was all perfectly proper. But Michael was rather a bad sport about it and his attitude infected my silly Shirley. After that, they liked to talk about my assets as being only held in trust for them. Morally, I mean. They were perfectly beastly about me taking taxis and travelling first class. So now you see why I took the opportunity to let them think that I wouldn't be long for this world.

Bruce I do.

Clemmie You seem rather quiet, Brucie dear.

Bruce (*sulkily*) One can't always be bubbling with fun.

Clemmie You're cross with me. Because I slightly misled you.

Bruce Well, you did rather break the rules of the engagement. It's not my job to escort healthy, sexually voracious women around Europe. I'm too old for such capers.

Clemmie Not at all, darling. You proved that last night.

Bruce That was a one-off. The point is that my professional expertise is in another area. Caring for desperately sick invalids.

Clemmie With healthy bank balances.

Bruce They are the only ones who can afford my fees.

Clemmie You haven't done so badly out of me. Though I'm afraid you will have to wait longer than you expected for that legacy.

Bruce It wasn't for myself.

Clemmie In the natural order of things, I can hardly last for more than twenty years. Simon will then only be thirty-three and Melissa thirty.

Bruce You know that will be too late. You've been teasing me all along.

Clemmie You rather invited it.

Bruce (*coldly*) A client's privilege, Mrs Wyndham-White.

Clemmie Oh, do cheer up. We'll have a slap-up dinner this evening, our last night.

Bruce I'm sorry. (*Miserably*) I was thinking about the poor young people.

Clemmie Which ones?

Bruce Mine. Thirty-three is no age to enter a school for gifted children.
Clemmie It could be forty-three. My mother lived to be over ninety.
Bruce Now you really are mocking me.
Clemmie You deserve it, darling. You're such a fraud yourself.
Bruce I don't know what you mean.
Clemmie Oh, yes, you do. My solicitor made a few enquiries. He's that kind of man. That's really why he rang back, You haven't got any children, have you? In fact you've been smart enough not to get married at all.
Bruce Oh, dear.
Clemmie It wouldn't have fooled anyone for long. But then a dying woman wouldn't have had long.
Bruce I'm afraid I have a creative mind. They spotted it at school.
Clemmie Shall we call it thirty all? A little deal on the Rialto, in which each side tried to do better than the other. We are both Venetians at heart, aren't we?
Bruce I seem to have lost out all along the line.
Clemmie Not at all, dear. I decided not to cancel my codicil. The fax arrived this very morning. I've already signed it and posted it back to London. Father's training, you know. So you can be sure of getting something in the end. So long as you survive me.
Bruce That was decent of you.
Clemmie Not at all. It was in gratitude. For making me believe I'm a desirable woman again. And perhaps it also appealed to my sense of the absurd.
Bruce I feel a bit small.
Clemmie That won't last long. Mind you, Bruce, I shall be wary of you in future. You might poison my soup.
Bruce Very funny.
Clemmie I'm looking forward to another night on the town.
Bruce There's a rarely performed baroque opera at the Fenice. With original instruments.
Clemmie That wasn't quite what I meant.
Bruce To be honest, I'm rather tired today.
Clemmie You were in splendid form last night. Like a wild thing with antlers.
Bruce That was the euphoria. I was so happy for the dear children.
Clemmie But they don't exist.
Bruce I forgot that. With all the excitement.

Clemmie suddenly gives a piercing scream. She makes a clumsy movement

Look out!

Sound of commotion. Excited comments from bystanders

Clemmie I almost went in.
Bruce Be careful. For heaven's sake.
Clemmie It was my own fault. I nearly went over the edge. Into the canal. So slippery.
Bruce It might have killed you.
Clemmie Very likely. The shock. The cold water. And the smell. I'm no spring chicken.
Bruce You shouldn't be out on your own.
Clemmie You may be right about that, darling. Thank you for putting your hand out to save me. And so promptly too. At least you're not into homicide. I'm glad I checked that.
Bruce (*lightly*) All part of the service.
Clemmie I should have mentioned. The codicil is curiously worded. A gimmick of my solicitor's. The sum you inherit is increased by twenty per cent for every year I live from today. Give me ten years and you will be quite rich. Even allowing for inflation. Provided I don't blow it all in my lifetime. Wouldn't that be naughty of me?
Bruce So you've offered me a vested interest?
Clemmie In my preservation. Yes. It's rather neat.
Bruce Then I shall have to look after you.
Clemmie That was my idea. You've got the perfect partner in me. I do a lot of voluntary work for private nursing homes. That means I can recruit wealthy invalids for you and we can cart them round Europe with a blank will form and a good quality fountain pen.
Bruce We?
Clemmie We're so well matched. You're a fraud by nature, dear. And so am I.
Bruce But you seemed so docile at first.
Clemmie People like that make the best frauds. We should be very happy together.
Bruce Together?

Clemmie I rather thought we might get married. I like to be considered respectable. Father was a brigadier.
Bruce I must have time to think.
Clemmie It will only be a quiet wedding. Shirley can be matron of honour. And I might ask Michael to give me away.
Bruce (*laughing*) Not bad for a dying lady.
Clemmie I'm longing to see the look on their faces.
Bruce Let's go back to the hotel.
Clemmie Oh, yes, please. A romp before dinner.
Bruce I would prefer to lie down. (*Faintly*) It's been an exhausting day. On top of a disturbed night.
Clemmie We'll take a gondola.
Bruce (*firmly*) Certainly not. We have to be careful with our money.
Clemmie It's only money, you know.
Bruce We need to make it last.

Fade out to the accompaniment of the sounds of Venice: the cries of gondoliers; hooting of steamers; babble of tourists and many bells; the Barcarolle again. All the din of the Rialto

CURTAIN

MORTMAIN

CHARACTERS

Diana
Steve

MORTMAIN

First presented on 15 January, 1992 at the King's Head Theatre, Islington by Sydney Golder for Elephant Theatre with the following cast:

Diana   Maggie Bourgein
Steve   Tim Shoesmith

Directed by Lynn Tilden

MORTMAIN

A middle-aged woman paces a room in a state of some agitation. She looks at a small diary which she has obviously studied many times before. She glances at her watch again and again. Then she pours herself a drink, not presumably the first. At last the bell rings and she goes to answer it. A young man enters. He too seems thoroughly strung up

Diana Do come in.
Steve Thanks.
Diana You must be...Steve...
Steve Yes. (*He pauses*)
Diana I'm Mrs Carter... of course...
Steve Yes.

They are very awkward with each other

Diana I'm afraid...I don't know your other name.
Steve May.
Diana It was good of you to come, Mr May...
Steve Least I could do...
Diana Do please sit down...

They sit

Steve Thank you.

There is a pause as each tries to think of something to say. The scene should be played with plenty of painful pauses

Diana I could have invited you to a restaurant...but it's harder to talk there...
Steve It was... better like this...
Diana You found your way all right...
Steve Swiss Cottage is not exactly...off the map.
Diana Would you like something to drink?
Steve I wouldn't mind...
Diana What will you have?
Steve What have you got?
Diana I've been drinking gin...and there's some kind of Spanish liqueur ... probably has a kick like a mule...it's my sister's flat, you see...I haven't had time to get things in...
Steve (*apprehensive*) Your sister: is she going to come back?
Diana Oh no, she's on holiday... rambling in Tuscany ... that's why I came to London now... to have somewhere handy to stay. (*She pauses*) It's not much fun... alone in a hotel...
Steve I understand...
Diana And to get away...
Steve Oh yes...You've had a hard time ...
Diana We still haven't decided...what you're going to drink...
Steve Same as you, please...I had one before...to get up my strength...
Diana I'll have a tiny drop more too...

She pours out generous drinks for them both

Steve (*tepidly*) Cheers.
Diana (*equally weakly*) Cheers. (*She pauses*) I had to see you...
Steve Yes...
Diana It's one of the main reasons...why I came over...
Steve Oh...
Diana Does that surprise you?
Steve It does a bit... I'm not so special...
Diana Yes, you are... you've played a special part in my life...
Steve (*defensive, slightly surly but not rude*) I expect you want me to say sorry... but I won't.
Diana I want more than that...
Steve I haven't got any money...
Diana Don't be silly... (*She pauses*)

Steve I suppose you're frightened...I might cause problems...sell my story to the tabloids...
Diana I was at first... but you've had weeks... I don't think you will now...
Steve (*ironically*) Thanks ever so much...
Diana I had to screw up my nerve... to ring you at all...
Steve It's not the first call I've had you know...from New York...
Diana (*sarcastically*) I'll bet... (*She pauses*)
Steve You hate me, don't you...?
Diana That's a hard question to answer...
Steve Don't try then...
Diana If you want an honest reply...I did hate you very much... at first...in the abstract...but it's not easy to sustain hatred for long...unless you've got a real talent for it...and then, when I rang you...I imagine I sounded rather bitchy...
Steve Not really...you seemed more... scared...
Diana Wouldn't anyone...I only had the name to go on... the Christian name... and the telephone number...the one I found in his diary...I wasn't even sure it was in London...I had no idea...who I might be talking to...what sort of man...
Steve Oh...
Diana I thought you might be crude... grasping... or perhaps terribly pansified...
Steve That's just ... stereotyped thinking...
Diana Maybe ... it's quite out of my experience... I half expected you to react negatively... but you just seemed ...shocked...
Steve Of course... I was shocked to hell...
Diana You mean... you didn't know...
Steve How could I... there was nobody to tell me... until you did...
Diana There were obituaries in *The Times* and the*Telegraph*... even though we had lived for so long in the States...
Steve I don't read those...
Diana I'm sorry now... I broke it like that...
Steve Not your fault, Mrs Carter...
Diana I realized you were genuinely upset... and that made me think you might be worth meeting... (*She pauses*) I'll be quite honest... I didn't ring you out of any friendly feeling... rather the opposite ... I was afraid you might make trouble ... my husband had quite a public reputation... it seemed best to tackle you head on... to find out how much you knew...

Steve Like... his surname...his real one...
Diana Well, yes...I didn't think he would have given you that... he was very discreet by nature...
Steve He happened ...to trust me ... (*He pauses*) Did you think I might be... a rent-boy?
Diana It did just cross my mind...
Steve Well, I'm not... (*He pauses*)
Diana You didn't sound...tough and worldly...on the phone. You seemed more... gentle...half-stunned... that was when I decided to try to meet you...
Steve What on earth for?
Diana I don't really know. I suppose...to try to understand...
Steve We can't change the past... he won't come back...
Diana No...but if you know why things happened, they can be easier to bear... There's one thing already...now that I actually see you... I don't think I shall be able to hate you any longer...
Steve (*sarcastically*) Very kind, I'm sure... (*He pauses*) I used to hate you too ... when Toby was buying those presents for you...all those books in Hatchards...burbling on about how you missed French cooking in the States...I knew he had something secure with you...from your young days together...something he would never quite have with me...there wouldn't be the time...
Diana You mean...you were jealous...
Steve I sure was...
Diana I hadn't thought of it...like that...(*She pauses*) There were other numbers in that diary... Mexico City, Toronto...
Steve Oh yes...Toby had his ports of call...
Diana He easily... became lonely...that travelling for the firm... getting the big accounts... deploying his charm... he was rather a charmer, wasn't he...
Steve He was the most charming person I have ever met...That was why it seemed so impossible... for him to be... dead... (*He pauses*)
Diana Yes...all that vitality... I'd like to call you Steve... if you don't mind...
Steve That's all right... (*He pauses*) He didn't, did he?
Diana He didn't what?
Steve He didn't... take his own life?
Diana What on earth... makes you think that?
Steve He always seemed to be... under tension... getting back to the hotel

for your calls...frightened that I might be cross with him...trying to please everyone...
Diana I know what you mean. For such a big jovial man...full apparently of the joy of life...my husband was... surprisingly unconfident... about his own lovableness... I think that's why I loved him so...
Steve You haven't given me an answer... (*He pauses*)
Diana It was a heart attack...
Steve (*suspiciously*) Very sudden...
Diana Heart attacks are...he was in the bath... The doctor said he might have had a weakness for years ... simmering away undetected... that was so typical of Toby ... he made all the rest of the firm have check-ups ... but he didn't bother himself...
Steve Perhaps he didn't want to know... he was a great one...for sweeping problems under the rug...
Diana That was his professional manner... you see, in the advertising business, it's very important to make the client feel confident... they like to be sure they're backing a winner... Toby became very American in that way...though our American friends always thought of us as...terribly British...
Steve Do you think... he was a completely happy man?
Diana Is there such a person? He got a lot of pleasure out of travel, food, bossing his staff around like a cheerful uncle...In his heart, he might have been a bit... desolate... quite a lot of people are... but he didn't want to die...if that's what you're getting at...
Steve I'm glad... you're so sure... (*Pause*)
Diana There are many things I want to ask you, Steve.
Steve Oh yes...
Diana How did you meet him?
Steve (*sarcastically*) Surprising, isn't it... us two getting together... him such a man of the world... me so insignificant...
Diana Please... don't be so touchy...
Steve If you want to know... it was in the store... that's where I work... I'm in men's shirts now...measuring necks...not always very clean...the necks, I mean...in those days I had been lent temporarily ... to Ladies Handbags...not a job for a man but it was an emergency... one of their dolly birds had eloped to the Gulf with a favoured customer...your husband came in to buy a present...for you...I thought he was very dishy...with that touch of grey hair...and he seemed to take to me...we had to keep it short...Miss Madrigal was looking at us out of the corner

of her eye... a real bitch, that woman... he asked me where I went after work... and I said the pub on the corner... *The Lucifer in Starlight* ...though I never did usually... well, I was there that evening... and so was he... (*He pauses*)... I knew he would be...
Diana (*dryly*) Congratulations...
Steve I'm not a tart, Mrs Carter... not even an enthusiastic amateur...
Diana Please, Steve... we mustn't quarrel... do call me... Diana...
Steve I'll never forget that evening... we talked and talked...
Diana Talked?
Steve Yes... does that surprise you? We did a lot of talking, Toby and me... you see, he could tell me everything...
Diana (*dryly*) I wouldn't be too sure of that. Toby tended to... compartmentalise his relationships... to put it charitably...
Steve All I know is... we felt OK together... nothing else mattered... I'm sorry... this can't be very nice for you...
Diana It's all right... I invited it...
Steve We talked until *The Lucifer* closed... and then... Well, I couldn't take him home... not to Mum and Dad... they'd have had a blue fit... Dad used to be in the Fire Service... so we had to go back to his hotel... right past that snooty man on the door... full marks to old Toby... he didn't bat an eyelid... kept waffling away about some papers I was supposed to be coming up to collect... luckily, I was wearing my business suit... we get them at a discount... but Toby didn't fool that commissionaire... high class chucker-outer, that's all he was... I happened to look back as we were waiting for the lift... the bastard gave me a wink... made me feel awful... (*He pauses*)
Diana I don't want to know... the rest... I'd prefer to remember... the other side of my husband...
Steve The butch, heterosexual side... yes, Toby worked hard on that... but it was never really... him...
Diana (*sharply*) Oh really? I lived with him for twenty years... I ought to know him by now... better than you... All you had were little flings.
Steve (*angered*) Christ, you're so conventional... they weren't little flings... as you like to call them... Toby and me... it was bloody marvellous...
Diana OK... you had a good time... but you knew all along... that there were other... friends... in other cities...
Steve So what? I wasn't married to the man... was I?
Diana I really don't understand... what you saw in him... such a difference in age...

Steve He was kind ... and generous...and good fun...we had lots of laughs ... but there was something more... he cared about me... remembered the things I told him... about my family...about the store...I felt I was somebody...when I was with him... nobody else has ever treated me like that...taken me seriously... (*He pauses*)

Diana (*quietly*) That was the Toby I knew too...

Steve He used to ring me from time to time...send me postcards... I longed for his visits to London...Why didn't you ever come too?

Diana Toby was always inviting me... he could have taken me anywhere... on the firm... but then, in the last years, he had to travel such a lot... bringing the business to New York... I couldn't keep stringing along...I have my own work, you see...

Steve Toby told me...aren't you with some high-powered law firm in Wall Street?

Diana Only as a bumped-up personal assistant...but I get to learn a bit of the jargon... that was why I didn't mind so much when Toby was away... and he didn't seem to mind either, going off on his own... (*dryly*) I discovered why...even when I came across those telephone numbers...and compared them with his earlier diaries... I realized that he had been seeing you regularly for nearly three years... every time he passed through London...it was all down... dates and times of meeting...no attempt to hide...he knew I wouldn't snoop...not when he was alive...and he didn't expect to die when he did...(*She pauses*) I felt...quite sick... (*She pauses*)

Steve Is that true?

Diana What?

Steve Your feeling sick...when you realized your husband had been seeing...men...

Diana It came as a terrible shock...

Steve Oh, come on...those telephone numbers might have meant nothing...old friends, business contacts...What made you jump to the conclusion...that I must be a boyfriend? (*He pauses*)

Diana That's a good question...(*she pauses*)...all right...I had never known consciously ... not with the front part of my mind...I wasn't a complacent wife... but when I found out there was this person called Steve...then it did sort of click into place... (*She pauses*)

Steve That's more... honest...I had the advantage, you see...I knew about you... from the start.

Diana Did he talk about me a lot?

Steve Yes...I got a bit sick of it... what a marvellous cook you were...and your superb taste in curtains...

Diana In a situation like that...many men would cheat...say their marriage had broken down...their wife didn't understand them...never their fault, of course...

Steve Toby didn't try that one...I knew he was always going back to you... he liked to be home for the weekend...to take you to that place, way out on Long Island...you'd never had children, so you needed him instead...

Diana (*dryly*) Is that how he put it? (*She pauses*) You tried hard to get him to leave me, I suppose?

Steve Not very hard...I knew it wouldn't work...Toby wouldn't have had the guts to live openly with another man...he cared too much about what other people might think...he always wanted to be popular...

Diana In the advertising industry...that's the whole point...(*She pauses*) Didn't he do anything for you?

Steve What d'you mean? He gave me presents...money from time to time...he never bought me a flat, if that's what you're getting at...I'm still living at home...it's not so cosy there any longer...now they've found out about me...Mum keeps cleaning the basin...and Dad's scared that his old mates will take the piss out of him at the local...

Diana I'm afraid...my husband left you nothing in his will...

Steve I didn't expect it...what do you think I am...? (*He pauses*)

Diana I still don't understand...why his death came as such a shock to you... it was a month before I rang you...during that time, you couldn't have heard from him...didn't that worry you?

Steve No. (*He pauses*) With Toby and me, it was always wonderful...every time we met...but we weren't exactly boy and girl sweethearts...he had to be careful... running that posh business... he rang me on birthdays...or to tell me he was coming to London...but it wasn't regular...

Diana I see. (*She pauses*) I suppose men aren't like women...in that way...

Steve That's what he liked in me...

Diana The real point is... where his heart lay...

Steve Does it matter now?

Diana It does...to me... you see, I *am* rather haunted by one question...was Toby fundamentally a homosexual who just about sustained his marriage to me ... with give and take on both sides...or was I the real centre of his life...and you and the others were... adventures on the side?

Steve You're silly to torture yourself...
Diana I'd like to know...whether my whole life was a sham or not...can you blame me? I know a lot of people are bisexual...but in the last analysis, you have to be one thing or the other... there's one sex that you dream about...
Steve I never asked Toby about his dreams... but I do think he may have found it easier to... deceive you with a boy... an area where you couldn't compete...
Diana He wouldn't have wanted to deceive me... but it must have been lonely for him... all those hotel bedrooms... I should have travelled with him more...
Steve It was more... fundamental... than that.
Diana I can see you want to believe that...You want to make your...little affair...into a great love...
Steve I want it to have some...dignity... (*He pauses*)
Diana Have another gin...
Steve Yes, please...

She pours drinks for both of them

Diana I must warn you, Steve...I'm not finding it easy to keep my cool...
Steve You should try working in a store...all that hassle... (*He pauses*)
Diana Toby owed me a lot, you know... and he never denied it...when we first went to the States, we didn't have money... and he needed a lot of encouragement... he wasn't nearly as confident as he pretended on the outside... but then he started to do well in his job...he developed a flair...a new sort of advertising for the Americans...a refreshing change from the usual super-hype...Toby hit on the idea of using British understatement instead...those two old men in their Club saying " not a bad little brandy "...the two pretty girls finding Toby's soap "just a shade cheaper" than its rivals...the novelty caught on...that's how Toby managed to start his own business...I nagged him into taking the risk. You know the rest...
Steve I still don't know... how you and he really got on...
Diana We were tremendous friends... and partners too... that's not...nothing, you know...On the physical side... we were both rather tired by the evenings...It didn't seem to matter...but perhaps I was wrong... perhaps he was yearning all the time...
Steve You must have had some idea...

Diana Now I come to think of it...he did sometimes stare rather wistfully at pretty young waiters...he was always one for beauty...he loved pedigree cats... (*She pauses*) Maybe you were a substitute...when he didn't have me.

Steve It wasn't like that at all...I gave him something he needed... you see, when a man has to be the boss, to give orders all day and then come back to a wife who expects him to take the lead, it's possible to develop a hankering after the opposite...a relationship where he lets someone else...take command...

Diana That doesn't sound like Toby...

Steve Not to you...but there was a side to him that you never saw...

Diana I'm not very interested...in the details. (*She pauses*) It seems so weird...you and my husband...

Steve It was a...complicated friendship.

Diana (*patronizing*) I expect something went wrong for you...when you were a child...

Steve I've never got on well with my dad...he's a good man...but he just doesn't understand.

Diana (*triumphantly*) As I thought...Toby was a substitute father.

Steve He encouraged me...that meant more to me than... anything else...

Diana (*pleased*) It's easier for me...to see it as a kind of friendship... between an older and a younger man...

Steve I know what you want...to sanitize me...to relegate me to being...just a protegé...but I was much more than that, Mrs Carter...and I loved Toby...and he was crazy about me. (*Working himself up*) He said he wanted to leave you and come to England and set up with me... but he couldn't bear to do it...you were a dependent wife... not young enough to change your lifestyle now... you'd never make it alone in New York... or anywhere else...

Diana (*coldly*) You had a narrow escape... he wasn't the faithful type... he had those other boys...

Steve Only for when he had to travel...he told me...

Diana He was stringing you along... using that fatal charm...I was the real partner...He was a normal man... you tried to make him into a queer... (*She pauses*)

Steve At least you're being honest now... you still hate me, don't you? (*He pauses*)

Diana Don't you hate me? (*She pauses*)

Steve I pity you.

Diana That's more offensive...than hatred...(*She pauses*)
Steve I shall go now. (*She pauses*)
Diana Look, Steve, we can't part like this...I shan't sleep a wink. I'm sorry about what I just said. It's been a terrible strain...for both of us. Don't you see... little though we may like it...we are linked by all that has happened. There's a mediaeval phrase that is still occasionally used in law...when something is held under posthumous control...they say it's in mortmain... in the grip of a dead hand... that's how we've been left, you and I... prisoners of our memories... but we have free will...we don't have to be enemies.
Steve All right...if you want it that way...but stop it then...trying to play me down. All my life, I've wanted to be taken seriously...and that's what Toby did for me.
Diana It seems we both...have reason to be grateful to him...and yet he got us all into a horrible mess... (*She pauses*) There's something else...
Steve Oh?
Diana I haven't told you everything yet...
Steve What do you mean? (*He pauses*)
Diana There was more in that diary...than just names and telephone numbers. Toby was up to something...shortly before his death...you know how he used to organize things...getting all the relevant information in advance... his blitzes, he used to call them. Well... he had collected telephone numbers for house agents...and for the top advertising firms... his professional skill would have been welcomed anywhere ... in the English speaking world. I'm virtually certain he was planning to sell up in New York and move away...without me... but he wouldn't have been alone...
Steve You can't prove that.
Diana I don't need to.
Steve Where would that have left you?
Diana (*bleakly*) Out in the cold...(*She pauses*) You must have had some idea...
Steve We did talk about it...from time to time...a kind of dream...we once looked at a marvellous little house...in one of those backwaters off the Fulham Road...backing on to the Brompton Cemetery...very secluded...lots of birds...
Diana (*sarcastically*) A sort of love-nest...
Steve It would have been peaceful...that's what he needed most...all that travelling...he was beginning to be burned out...but I told you...I didn't

think he would have the guts...to leave you...
Diana (*ironically*) It would seem...he was trying to screw up his courage... (*She pauses*)
Steve Well, it doesn't matter now, does it? Toby isn't going anywhere. (*Sharply*) That diary...did you look at it when he was still alive...?
Diana Maybe I did...now I come to think of it...
Steve It must have made you... bloody mad...Didn't you have it out with him?
Diana I was frightened...of getting the wrong answer... Besides, I was used to poor Toby's pipe-dreams...he once took me to view a broken down mansion on a cliff in upstate New York...with spectacular views over the Hudson River...he always wanted to be somewhere different...and in other company...
Steve Talking to you...it's like peeling an onion, isn't it?... layers of truth have to be stripped away...I think you were jealous as hell... didn't you feel like murder?
Diana Don't be so silly, Steve... I loved the man, in spite of his faults...I'd never kill anybody...
Steve Anyone could commit murder... if they felt strongly enough...I would have killed for Toby...and I still could...don't smile like that, please...if I seem meek and mild, that's how they like us in the store...ultra polite...it's excruciating sometimes...(*He pauses*)
Diana Let's try to see this in perspective...Toby loved us both...I accept that now...it's not really so strange...you know how he was...gregarious, affectionate... best in company...he loved very easily...too easily...and then he got bored...that was the danger point...
Steve I know...that's why I just tried to be happy...while it lasted...Nothing good ever lasts...at least, not with me...
Diana Don't give way...to self-pity...it's terribly corrosive...

She puts her hands on his sleeve and pauses

Steve I can't make you out...Diana. You seem to be making an effort to be...quite nice to me. But then you keep getting in...bitchy digs...
Diana I'm only human... (*She pauses*)
Steve What are you going to do now?
Diana See a few shows in London...and then go back to New York...I have friends there and the job...I don't suppose I shall be back in London for some time...

Steve I see... (*He pauses*) I shan't get higher than Men's Shirts... I failed the management course...they said I had the brains... but I would always be looking in from the outside...
Diana It was kind of you to give up your free time...
Steve Least I could do...
Diana I enjoyed meeting you...
Steve No, you didn't...and I don't blame you...
Diana All right...I'll try to be completely frank... one side of me does still dislike you...I begrudge all those hours you spent with my Toby...the laughter, the fun he might have had with me...
Steve I know what he would have liked...for us three to be together... a bit of a joke really...
Diana A ménage à trois... rather humiliating for me... but I believe they *can* work, strange though it may seem...
Steve It's not strange...if you understand that love and sex aren't the same thing... Toby taught me that...
Diana He taught us both... quite a lot...I think we have to come to terms with that... we both have these memories...Toby holds us in his dead hand...(*She pauses*) I brought you something...(*She fumbles in her bag*)
Steve (*dead-pan*) You're not getting out...a gun, are you?
Diana (*amused*) My dear Steve...you've been watching too much television...
Steve (*sullen*) In our house...there's nothing much else to do ...
Diana You'd better look for...another Toby then.
Steve They don't grow...on every tree. (*He pauses*)
Diana (*finally producing something from her bag*) I wanted you to have this...Toby's lighter...
Steve Good grief...it's too classy for me...solid silver...I've watched him use it so often...
Diana That's why you should have it... as a memento. (*She pauses*)
Steve You don't have to give me... anything at all...
Diana Shall we call it...a peace-offering?
Steve You brought it from the States...specially for me?
Diana I brought it just in case...in case we managed to establish some kind of human contact...I do hope we have...
Steve (*slowly*) Thank you very much...Diana... (*clearly touched*)...it was a nice idea ...Toby cared so much about you...he hated the thought of you having to suffer... that's what tore him apart...towards the end...

Diana Let's stop then...tearing him apart again...disputing about his affection for each of us... (*She pauses*)
Steve All right... bury the hatchet...
Diana There was something of a parent's love in Toby's feeling for you...you can't deny that...I could be part of it...why don't you come and have a week or two with me in New York...I'll pay your expenses...
Steve That's very kind of you...very generous...I'll think about it...I can't say, yes at once...it seems a strange idea...I've often thought about your life there... hoping you would die...
Diana I'm ravenous... let's go out now to dinner... and I'll pay, of course...
Steve No, I'll take you...I got my pay cheque yesterday...
Diana Don't be ridiculous...Toby left me the company...I'm quite rich...
Steve Poor people have their pride, you know...tonight it's on me...I'm sorry if I've been a bit...unfriendly...I hadn't realized it would be like this...
Diana Nor had I. (*She pauses*) You're an unusual young man...
Steve I've had some... unusual experiences...

They get ready to go out

Diana You'd better let me know fairly soon... about New York. I've got to fit in another short trip...
Steve Oh?
Diana To Toronto...Jerry's his name...from the diary too...
Steve Why bother?
Diana It seems important...
Steve Toby did mention him... quite casually. (*He pauses*)
Diana I'm afraid you misunderstood, Steve... I'm so sorry...
Steve What are you talking about?
Diana When I told you about all that research in Toby's diary... the preparations to move...you just assumed it was to London...
Steve (*fearfully*) Well...yes...
Diana He wasn't coming to London at all, Steve... he was going to Toronto... (*She pauses*)
Steve Why the hell are you telling me this? It's so bloody ... cruel ...
Diana (*an ambiguous smile*) I wanted to help you ... to remove that dead hand...

Black-out

DEAD END

CHARACTERS

Arabella Snelgrove
Brian Wedmore
Mother (voice only)

A small English country cottage

DEAD END

First presented on May 27, 1991 by Sydney Golder at the King's Head for Elephant Theatre with the following cast:

Arabella Snelgrove Gemma Page
Brian Wedmore Bruce Richardson

Directed by Michael Cullen

DEAD END

Arabella and Brian are talking in her cottage. She is a single woman, still attractive. Brian is in his thirties. They could be about the same age

Arabella I'm so glad you like it here.
Brian It's gorgeous ... so peaceful.
Arabella So typically English, I always think. Nothing could ever happen.
Brian But it's not dull.
Arabella Oh, no. Not if you care for gardening.
Brian It was lucky I stopped to admire your roses.
Arabella I could see you were a connoisseur.
Brian I'm not that. I'm just fond of the smell ... and the colour. Deep red is my favourite.
Arabella You were staring in such an interested way. That was what made me invite you to come in.
Brian You'd better be careful. There are some bad eggs around.
Arabella I'm sure I can trust you. You have an honest face.
Brian Some of the worst are like that ... the charming psychopaths.
Arabella I wanted you to enjoy the cottage.
Brian It's frightfully olde-worlde. The brass knobs ... the oak beams ... and the ingle-nook.
Arabella More my mother's taste than mine.
Brian Will I have the pleasure of meeting her?
Arabella I'm afraid not. She seldom sees anyone these days. And now what can I offer you? A cup of tea?
Brian I'd prefer sherry ... if it's equally convenient.
Arabella Of course.

She pours the drinks

Brian How kind you are.
Arabella It's a pleasure to offer hospitality. The village is such a show piece. We want visitors to enjoy themselves.

Brian You can afford to say that. You're miles from a town. That preserves you from the horrors of mass tourism.
Arabella I suppose you're right. We *are* rather off the beaten track.
Brian And your road here doesn't lead anywhere.
Arabella It's a cul-de-sac ... a dead end. And mine is the last house.
Brian You don't occasionally feel lonely?
Arabella Not really. Mother may be physically decrepit. But she has a lively mind.
Brian I'm awfully sorry to miss her.
Arabella She still keeps in touch with the world. Through me.
Brian I gather she was once quite a power in the land here ... Women's Institute ... drama group.
Arabella (*surprised*) Oh, you know about Mother?
Brian They told me in the village. I got chatting.
Arabella I can see you're the type.
Brian What type?
Arabella To get chatting.
Brian Talkative, you mean?
Arabella No, friendly.
Brian Thank you, Miss ... er...
Arabella Arabella Snelgrove. It's a silly name, I'm afraid. But I didn't invent it.
Brian I'm Brian Wedmore.
Arabella Married, I suppose?
Brian No.
Arabella Nor am I.
Brian It's a pity your mother can't get out more.
Arabella She does go sometimes.
Brian She's never seen in the village.
Arabella How do you know?
Brian They told me.
Arabella Mother takes little walks after dark.
Brian How strange. Why is that?
Arabella She doesn't like people looking at her.
Brian Self-conscious, perhaps?
Arabella In a way.
Brian That's funny. She used to run the Women's Institute. They must have looked at her then.
Arabella She has changed. She's quite old, you know.

Brian Fading mentally, maybe?
Arabella Not in the least. Just withdrawing a bit.
Brian How long is it since anyone saw her? Other than yourself?
Arabella A little time, I suppose.
Brian Three or four years, they said.
Arabella It could be that.
Brian You would expect the doctor to call.
Arabella She doesn't want him. She's not ill. Being elderly is not an illness. You'll find that out yourself one day ... if you live to be old.
Brian Doesn't he try to come, all the same?
Arabella Yes, but she won't have him.
Brian It only takes a skip of the heart beat. If anything happened, it would be awkward. For the doctor, I mean.
Arabella I don't see why.
Brian He should have examined her. It would help with the Death Certificate.
Arabella That hasn't arisen yet.
Brian It must be inconvenient sometimes. Your mother refusing to go out in the daytime. For example, I suppose she's entitled to some form of pension. How does she draw that?
Arabella It comes by post.
Brian Aren't there sometimes things to sign?
Arabella I do that for her. Her fingers are a bit unreliable. Nobody seems to mind.
Brian They might mind.
Arabella Mind what?
Brian If things were wrong.
Arabella What could be wrong?
Brian Nowadays there is a lot of fraud, I'm afraid. People claiming benefits they're not entitled to.
Arabella But of course Mother is entitled to a pension. In fact she has three.
Brian Three?
Arabella There's the pension from the State... everyone gets that. Then there's a pension from my late father's company. And Mother also receives an annuity. She bought it with her savings.
Brian They all die with her?
Arabella I suppose so.
Brian That will be a sad day for you.

Arabella Well, of course.
Brian I was thinking of the loss of the three pensions.
Arabella I should be all right. I would be free to take a job then. And I have a bit of money of my own ... and some good jewellery. It was left by an aunt.
Brian How fortunate.
Arabella My sister wasn't at all pleased at the time. Mind you, she was twenty years older than me.
Brian As much as that?
Arabella Yes, my father had been based abroad. Soon after he retired at fifty, I was born. My mother was over forty and my sister was already married.
Brian I see.
Arabella I'm afraid I was always spoilt, so when my aunt died and left me the jewellery, my sister said it ought to have been divided. She's dead now, poor thing. We rather lost touch. The family didn't much care for her husband.
Brian So you have no other relations?
Arabella I've got a nephew ... my sister's son. He can't be much younger than me. He lives in the North. I haven't seen him since we were children. I shouldn't recognize him if I met him now.
Brian What a pity he can't come and see you.
Arabella I don't know that I should like that. When he was a boy he used to do ... well ... rather cruel things.
Brian He's still your flesh and blood.
Arabella I suppose so. Anyway, the family feud will be made up one day. I've left my nephew everything I possess. It seemed only fair.
Brian But you could get married?
Arabella I don't think so. But even if I did, I feel my aunt's legacy should go to my nephew. He'll have to wait for it a long time, I hope.
Brian I'm glad you've got a bit of money.
Arabella Why is that, Mr Wedmore?
Brian It helps to allay suspicion.
Arabella I don't understand.
Brian You know how tongues wag in a village.
Arabella I don't really. We keep rather aloof ... because of Mother.
Brian That's the point. She's never seen. How do they know she is still alive?
Arabella It's none of their business.

Brian They think it is ... at the Post Office, even though the pension comes by post. There are stringent penalties for concealing a death. It would be fraudulent to go on drawing the pension after that.

Arabella But of course. I should never think of doing so.

Brian We live, unfortunately, in an age of suspicion.

Arabella (*annoyed*) So it would seem.

Brian Few of us are entirely above board.

Arabella Speak for yourself, Mr Wedmore.

Brian Take me for example. What do you think I am? Poet? Painter? Pianist?

Arabella A minor civil servant.

Brian Absolutely right. I'm a man from the Ministry. We don't wear bowler hats anymore. I left my briefcase in the car.

Arabella There's no car outside.

Brian Other side of the common. I thought it would be more tactful. One is trained to be tactful. Right from the start.

Arabella So you came here on purpose?

Brian If you hadn't invited me in, I should have knocked on the door. A firm but unterrifying knock is what the training manual advises.

Arabella I thought you were asking some pertinent questions.

Brian Better than being impertinent. (*He chuckles feebly*) I have these flashes of wit.

Arabella What is your ministry, may I ask?

Brian The Department of Health and Social Security.

Arabella (*naïvely*) Oh, you're awfully nice fellows. Mother's State pension comes from you.

Brian (*ominously*) Exactly.

Arabella How nice that you can now see for yourself how well the money is being spent!

Brian That was my intention.

Arabella I think that's rather touching. Using your day off in this way. It quite restores my faith in human nature.

Brian But it's not my day off. If it was, I should be wearing my country shirt and my natty jeans.

Arabella You mean they pay you to come and drink sherry with me.

Brian In a way. I'm an investigator.

Arabella How thrilling! A sort of detective.

Brian You could say that. My job is to look into cases of suspected fraud.

Arabella (*composed*) A snooper?

Brian It's not a word we favour.
Arabella It can't be everyone's cup of tea. More sherry, by the way?
Brian No, thank you.
Arabella Well, I hope you're not investigating me.
Brian That *was* my plan. I want to be sure that your mother is still alive.
Arabella You *can* be sure. I give you my word.
Brian That's not quite enough.
Arabella I find that rather sad and insulting too. I'm a Friend of the Victoria and Albert Museum and my uncle went to Charterhouse. You'd do better to call on Major Pawson-Smith at the Old Forge. Ask him about his television licence.
Brian It's proof about your mother that we need.
Arabella How long have you entertained these unworthy suspicions?
Brian About a year.
Arabella You should have sent someone before.
Brian We did.
Arabella Well? What was the report?
Brian There wasn't one.
Arabella How strange! and how unlike the Civil Service.
Brian It was a mix-up, somehow. They do happen occasionally. Our Mr Marlow was due to visit you on a Friday afternoon. It was too late for him to report back that night. Next week he was joining another ministry in Scotland. He wanted to make a clean break.
Arabella He could have reported from Scotland.
Brian He could ... but he didn't. We sent reminders. They must have been pigeon-holed. Mr Marlow was like that. We weren't sorry to lose him.
Arabella You could have tried again.
Brian We did ... fresh blood. Mr Ross-Trimmingham ... A retired diplomat ... tremendously urbane. The iron hand in the velvet glove.
Arabella Couldn't he clear up the mystery?
Brian Far from it ... He became one himself. He just threw everything up.
Arabella Oh, dear ... How messy.
Brian I mean, he resigned. We never saw him again. A typewritten postcard arrived saying he had gone to Tasmania ... in a sailing boat ... alone. Of course, when you met Mrs Ross-Trimmingham, you could understand why.
Arabella You could have asked him for a report.
Brian He didn't leave a forwarding address.
Arabella Then he won't get a pension.

Brian (*nastily*) That seems to mean a lot to you.
Arabella How strange! Losing two men in that way. Like the brides in the bath.
Brian I don't see the connection.
Arabella *They* kept disappearing too. Eventually people began to wonder.
Brian We're too busy for abstract speculation. A sense of wonder is not encouraged in Whitehall. But we would like to know what you remember about these visitors. You were their last port of call.
Arabella I don't remember them at all.
Brian How odd! One could perhaps forget Mr Marlow ... a rather ordinary person. But Mr Ross-Trimmingham had a touch of the exotic. I believe he had served in Brussels. (*He pauses*) There's one other thing I should like to ask.
Arabella Go on.
Brian (*sharply*) Why does your garden contain three freshly dug graves?
Arabella (*sweetly*) I thought you might enquire about them. They belong to my boxers ... such dears. There's no more soothing lullaby to me than the heavy breathing of a boxer.
Brian Pugilists?
Arabella Dogs.
Brian They died together?
Arabella It was something in the stew ... not one of my best.
Brian The graves look too big.
Arabella They were big boxers.
Brian Who dug the graves?
Arabella I did ... of course.
Brian But you're fragile.
Arabella I have surprisingly strong muscles in my wrists. It always gives... people a surprise.
Brian It seems strange ... three dogs dying like that.
Arabella There were only two.
Brian Two? Well then ... What was the other grave for?
Arabella I thought I would get it ready ... while I was about it. Animals die here in the woods ... one wants to be prepared. And now might I ask you a tiny question?
Brian With pleasure.
Arabella Did you come alone?
Brian Well, yes. You see, I'm on my way home. I'm going on holiday

tomorrow.
Arabella So your office won't be expecting you back?
Brian Not for three weeks.
Arabella I suppose they know where you are now?
Brian Damn! I meant to leave a note. Perhaps I could telephone from here?
Arabella (*sweetly*) I'm afraid it's out of order.

She goes to a drawer and takes out a large hammer

Brian What have you in mind, Miss Snelgrove?
Arabella If you disappeared today, nobody would even know where you had been. And you wouldn't even be missed for some time.
Brian I suppose not.

She advances upon him, with uplifted hammer

Arabella It's always a good idea to let someone know where you've gone. In case anything happens.
Brian I wish I had.
Arabella Things *can* happen, you know, even in a quiet place like this. A real dead end.

She uses the hammer to knock down the edge of the carpet. Then she calmly leaves it on the table

Arabella That carpet is always annoying me.
Brian (*mopping his brow*) I ought to be getting on. I feel rather exhausted.
Arabella But you've got no answers to your questions.
Brian I have enough to go on, thank you. Quite enough.
Arabella I'm enjoying our chat. Sometimes I feel I ought to meet more people. I shouldn't like to get peculiar.
Brian Something tells me I really must go. I don't want anything unpleasant to happen ... for both our sakes.
Arabella You must just stay for five minutes longer and have a glass of my special redcurrant wine.

She turns her back on him and pours out wine with various motions of the hands

Brian Redcurrant wine. We used to enjoy it so when we were children. But I thought I'd had my last glass.
Arabella (*sweetly*) Here it is.
Brian Won't you join me?
Arabella It will be more fun just to watch you.

Brian raises his glass slowly

Brian A slightly bitter bouquet.
Arabella Drink it up. It will make you feel quite different.

Mother's voice is suddenly heard, calling loudly from upstairs

Mother (*off*) Arabella! Arabella! Who the hell have you got down there?

Brian looks surprised

Arabella (*seeing the surprise on Brian's face*) Oh, my dear Mr Wedmore you didn't seriously think, did you, that Mother was dead and I'd murdered your friends? How perfectly idiotic!
Brian Don't laugh at me. I don't like it.
Arabella Major Pawson-Smith will be most amused.
Brian (*getting furious*) I warn you. I can't take it.
Arabella (*merrily*) You really are rather silly. (*She burst into peals of laughter*)
Brian (*enraged*) Not half as silly as you are.

He suddenly seizes the hammer and hits her violently on the head. She falls to the ground

   Goodbye... Auntie Arabella!

Black-out

RIALTO

FURNITURE AND PROPERTY LIST

On stage: A café table
              Chairs

LIGHTING PLOT

Property fittings required: nil
Exterior

To open: General exterior lighting

Cue 1   **Bruce:**" We need to make it last."   (Page 17)
        Fade to black-out

EFFECTS PLOT

Cue 1   To open   (Page 1)
        Sounds of Venice as text page 1. Lively café

Cue 2   **Brian:** " ...show business nowadays"   (Page 5)
        A hoot as a vaporetto passes. Watery gurgles. Music

Cue 3   When ready   (Page 5)
        Cut music

Cue 4   When ready   (Page 5)
        Seagulls on the Venetian lagoon

Cue 5   **Clemmie:** "... go the whole hog."   (Page 9)
        *Sounds of the sea, children playing in the sand,
        a band in the distance*

Cue 6	**Brian**: " …forward to the wine."	(Page 12)
	Romantic music swells	
Cue 7	When ready	(Page 12)
	Steamers on the Grand Canal	
Cue 8	**Brian**: "Look out!"	(Page 16)
	Commotion, excited comments from bystanders	
Cue 9	Lights fade	(Page 17)
	Sounds of Venice	

MORTMAIN

FURNITURE AND PROPERTY LIST

On stage: Small diary
Bottle of gin
Glasses
Sofa
Handbag containing a silver lighter

Personal: **Diana**: wrist-watch (worn throughout)

LIGHTING PLOT

Property fittings required: nil
Interior

To open: Full general lighting

Cue 1	**Diana**: "… that dead hand…" *Black-out*	(Page 33)

EFFECTS PLOT

Cue 1	**Diana** pours herself a drink *Doorbell rings*	(Page 20)

DEAD END

FURNITURE AND PROPERTY LIST

On stage: Bottle of sherry
Sherry glasses
A table. *In a drawer*: a large hammer
Wine decanter
Chairs

LIGHTING PLOT

To open: General interior lighting

Cue 1 **Brian**: " … Goodbye… Auntie Arabella. " (Page 44)
Black-out

EFFECTS PLOT

No cues

www.ingramcontent.com/pod-product-compliance
Ingram Content Group UK Ltd.
Pitfield, Milton Keynes, MK11 3LW, UK
UKHW021842140426
5217IPUK00022B/1555